To: 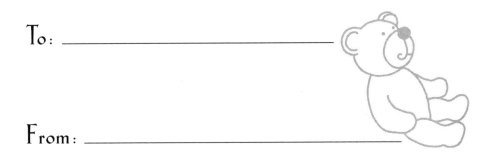_____

From: _____

Other books by Gregory E. Lang:

Why a Daughter Needs a Dad

Why a Son Needs a Dad

Why I Love Grandma

Why I Love Grandpa

Why a Son Needs a Mom

Why a Daughter Needs a Mom

Why I Chose You

Why I Love You

WHY I NEED YOU

100 reasons

GREGORY E. LANG

with photographs by Janet Lankford-Moran

CUMBERLAND HOUSE

NASHVILLE, TENNESSEE

Published by
Cumberland House Publishing, Inc.
431 Harding Industrial Drive
Nashville, TN 37211

Cover design: Unlikely Suburban Design
Text design: Lisa Taylor
Photographs and cover photo: Janet Lankford-Moran

Printed in Canada
1 2 3 4 5 6 7 8 — 09 08 07 06 05

To Mom and Dad, and my child, Meagan,
for all that you do.
—Greg

To John, for your tireless support
and belief in me.
—Janet

INTRODUCTION

Perhaps the most joyous moment of my life was when I held my newborn daughter for the first time. A nurse held her out to me, wrapped snug in a receiving blanket, in the world for only a few minutes. I eagerly but cautiously reached out and accepted her, taking great care to support her with both hands without holding her too tight, bringing her close to my chest to make sure I did not drop her, but not so close as to smother her. I spoke to her, in a near whisper, not wanting to startle her. "I love you," I said, before leaning down to kiss her forehead. Her sweet smell filled my lungs, her skin warmed my lips, and her cooing delighted my heart. In that moment my life changed forever.

In addition to that momentous day, I have had many other memorable moments with my little girl, like watching her take her first steps, the time she grabbed me by the ears and pulled my face toward hers before slobbering all over my nose, the afternoon that we crawled through winding tubes filled with plastic balls, chasing each other until our knees were sore, and my favorite, the first time she called me "Daddy." Nearly every day was fun and exciting, and yet nearly every day was challenging and at times stressful for her mother and me.

She was our only child, and although we thought we had prepared ourselves well for her arrival, I was fearful nonetheless, wondering if she was comfortable in my arms, was she wrapped too snugly, was she hungry or sleepy? I had watched my mother take care of my younger siblings, and my aunts take care of my many younger cousins. My wife and I read books to educate ourselves about infants, we listened to family and friends as advice based on experience was given, and we took home and saved all the instructions the pediatrician gave us. Still, sometimes we didn't know what to do, so we learned by trial and error, trying to read facial expressions, interpret baby jabber, remember schedules, and anticipate what need might arise next. We were afraid we would do something wrong, we feared causing some long-lasting harm, and we struggled with our confidence on difficult days when we could not please our unhappy child.

There were times when we wondered out loud what she needed from us, when we disagreed about what to do, and when we tried anything we could think of to handle the challenge of the moment. There were times when I doubted my abilities as a parent, when I wondered if my daughter would turn out all right, having been raised in part by me. There were times when I wanted desperately for her just to speak to me, to *tell* me what it was that she needed.

Those were the days that I wished she had come with a book, a parent's manual that described all possible infant behaviors and noises, reasons for tears, how to stop a runny nose, explanations for the different colors of poop and what to do for each one. Such a manual would have saved me a lot of frustration and doubt, a few temper tantrums (thrown by the both of us), and perhaps made my daughter a bit more content with her father. But alas, no such book existed.

I have tried to be a perfect parent. I have taken her to most of the places she wanted to go, bought all the stuffed animals that would fit in her room, given her the snacks she demanded even though I didn't want her to have them, and read to her at night long after she could read for herself. But I have not done everything right. I have fallen short more times than I can count.

Fortunately, I learned a few things from my successes as well as my mistakes and from the insights her mother shared with me. I learned that children are loving, resilient, and forgiving, but they are also delicate and impressionable. They will forgive us for most of our mistakes as long as our intentions were well placed and we do better the next time, but they cannot thrive in the face of indifference, carelessness, or anger. I learned that children have many needs that require the purposeful service of a devoted parent. While some of these needs are real only during early childhood, others endure for a lifetime and are staggering in their importance and effect if unattended. Some needs change, evolve, become less pressing, and others grow in importance as time goes by. Some needs must be met only once; others are never met but require constant feeding. Our children's own sense of worth is determined in large part by the worth they believe we have placed on them, which is demonstrated by how attentive we are to their needs rather than our own.

Our children will likely become parents themselves one day, will face the same questions we had when they were infants, and they will treat their own children as we treated them when they were our babes in arms. They will look back at their experiences with us to decide how to conduct themselves as parents. Their ability to parent will be directly related to the kind of parenting they received. Their ability to love their own child and to express that love freely and in abundance will be because we first loved them in that way. We will have done our jobs well if our child-turned-parent understands without us having to tell him or her that enduring sleepless nights, having endless patience, showing uncompromising love, and sacrificing without the promise of rewards are both the obligations and the pleasures of parenting.

Of course, my now-teenage child cannot recall all the care that I have given her, yet she knows of it. That is why now and then she calls me into her room at bedtime for a good-night hug, or reaches for my arm when we cross a parking lot, or calls me on the phone in near bursting exuberance to tell me about something she has conquered that day. These are the moments when I am rewarded for what I did years ago; these are *more* of the moments, like those of her infancy and early childhood, that I will remember for all of my days. These are the moments when I can smile and believe that her mother and I have done a pretty good job as her parents.

I never did find that manual, so I decided to write one. I do not hold this book out as the exhaustive book of wisdom that all new parents need to read in order to raise perfect children. However, I believe that somewhere there are parents lying awake at night, as my child's mother and I once did, wondering what to do for their beloved baby. I hope that by sharing a bit about what I have learned, about giving a child a loving, supportive start in life, about taking care of a few basic, universal needs, those parents will find confidence in their abilities, comfort in their successes, and strength with each life lesson shared with their child. With this book I hope to give new parents a glimpse of what they should know about and do for their young children, starting as soon as possible.

WHY I NEED YOU

I need you

to remember that I am watching everything you do.

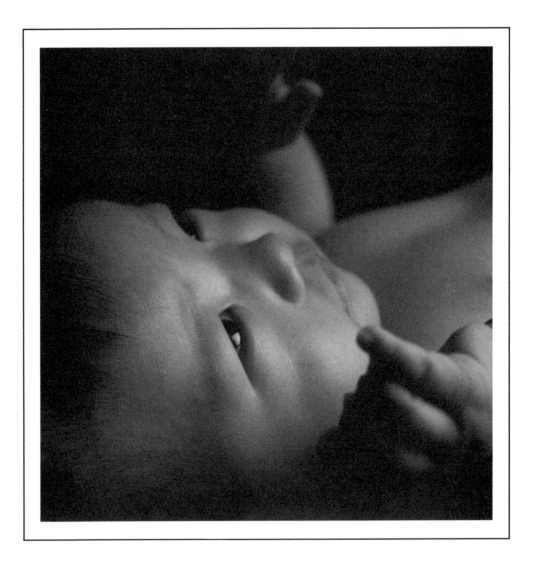

I need you

to know that the most comforting voice
in the world to me is yours.

I need you

to set an example for me as I grow up.

I need you . . .

to never stop loving me.

to rub my back when I don't feel well.

to keep my stuffed animals nice and clean.

to consider Grandma's advice. After all,
she has done this before.

I need you

to get me to eat the yucky stuff that is good for me.

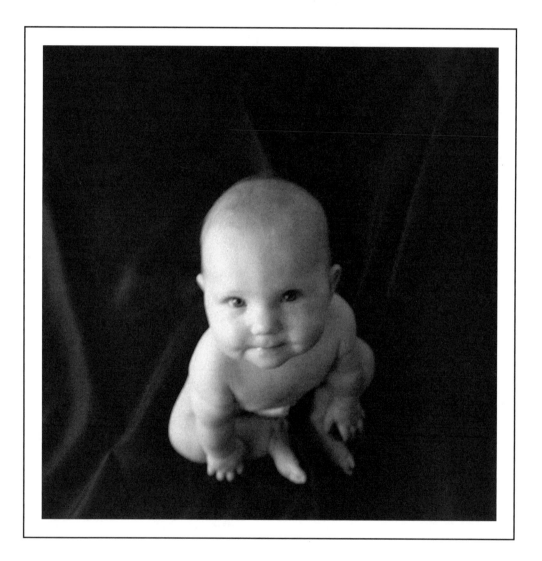

I need you

to prepare yourself for the changes
I am sure to go through.

I need you . . .

to make sure Santa Claus knows about me.

to remember to pack my blankie when we leave the house.

to help me learn how to count.

to carry me on your shoulders now and then.

I need you

to always remember that I am only a child.

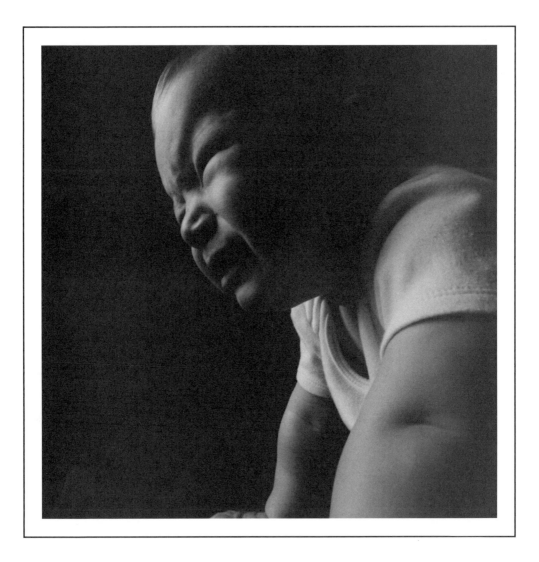

I need you

to be patient with me when I am frustrated.

I need you . . .

to sing my favorite songs to me.

to play peek-a-boo with me.

to make sure I am always snug in my car seat.

to make sure I don't eat dirt.

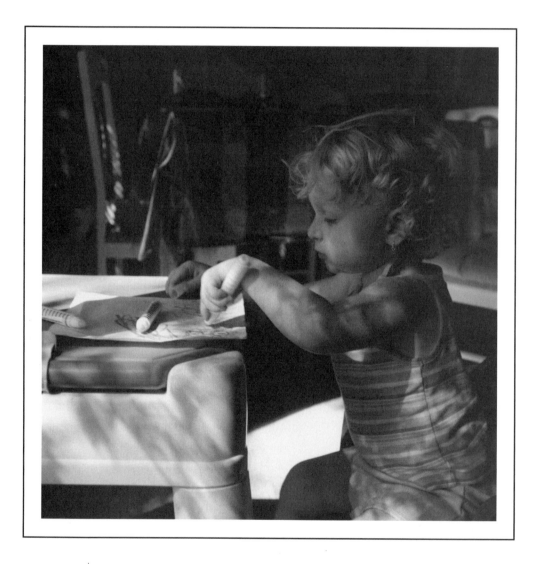

I need you

to make sure my toys are just right for me.

I need you

to teach me all that you know.

I need you

to make sure my bathwater isn't too hot.

I need you

to make time to play with me every day.

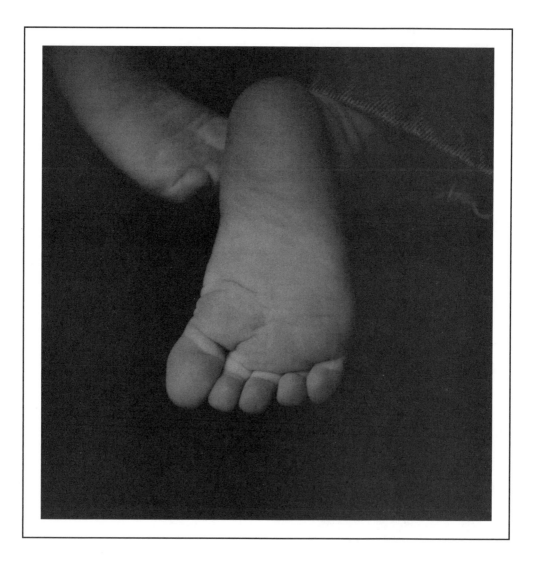

I need you

to keep the things I shouldn't have out of my reach.

I need you

to understand that for a while things aren't going to be as
neat and orderly as they once were.

I need you . . .

to carefully follow my doctor's instructions.

to always be ready to catch me if I fall.

to make sure I don't eat too much candy.

to pick me up when I reach for you.

I need you

to believe that you cannot spoil me too much.

I need you

to introduce me to our family traditions.

I need you

to remember that sometimes the simple pleasures
are the most fun.

I need you

to make sure I have lots of playmates.

I need you . . .

not to hover too much—I need to take
chances now and then.

to praise me when I do something the right way.

to rock me to sleep once in a while.

to speak to me in a soft, slow voice.

I need you

to encourage me when I try to do new things.

I need you

to remember that I want to be included in everything.

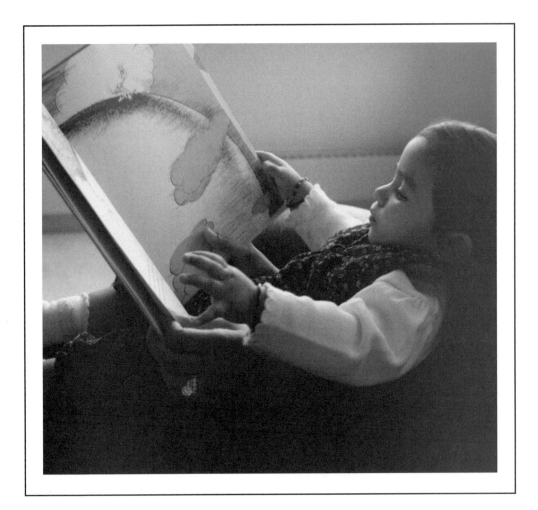

I need you

to read to me often.

I need you . . .

to let me grow up—I can't be a baby forever.

to make sure I learn good manners.

to help me understand why I can't always have my way.

to always accept my affection.

I need you

to understand that I cannot tell time.
To me everything is "now."

I need you

to protect me from the weather.

I need you . . .

to keep a watchful eye on me.

to comfort me when I am afraid.

to kiss me often.

to understand that I didn't intend to awaken you,
I just missed you.

I need you

to keep me clean and smelling fresh.

I need you

to carry me when I am tired.

I need you

to take me outside and explore the world with me.

I need you . . .

to make sure I have plenty of toys!

to teach me to share my toys with others.

to find me a really fun babysitter.

to avoid giving me an embarrassing nickname.

I need you

to remember that I like things to be predictable.

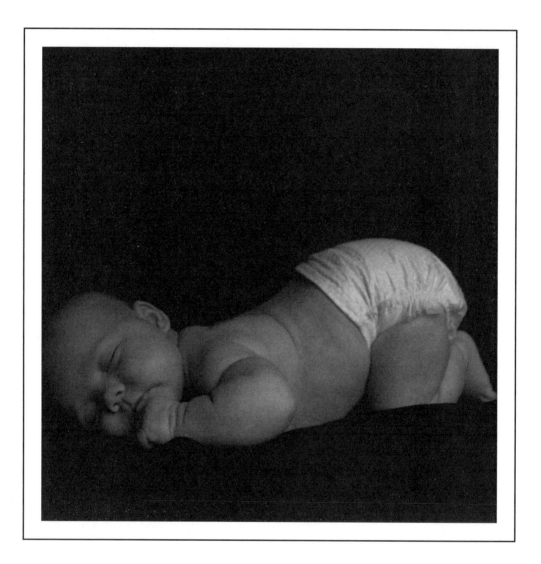

I need you

to make sure I don't skip my naps.

I need you

to introduce me to everyone in our family.

I need you

to learn my language until I can speak yours.

I need you

to remember that my feelings can be easily hurt.

I need you

to reassure me that you are glad I am here.

I need you . . .

to prepare yourself for how your life will
change with me in it.

to understand that sometimes all I know to do is to cry.

to remember that there are some things
that I am just too young to see.

to understand that while you might be tired of it, I'm thrilled
to do it again. And again. And again.

I need you

to remember where I left my favorite toy.

I need you

to snuggle with me often.

I need you

to tickle me, but not too much.

I need you . . .

to let me hold your hand whenever I want to.

to take a nap with me once in a while.

to resist taking embarrassing photographs of me.

to resist dressing me in weird outfits.

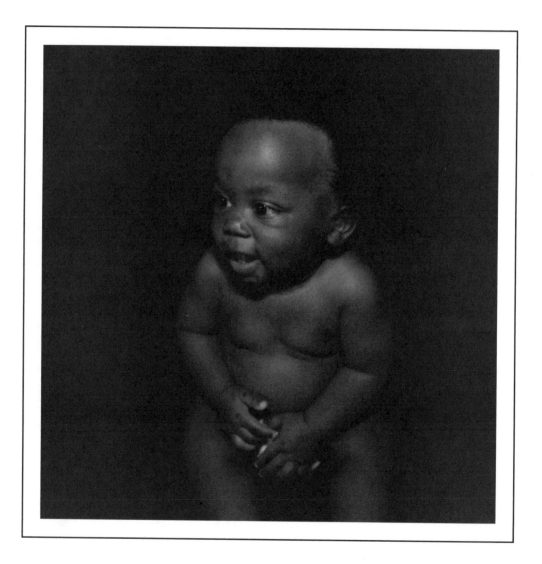

I need you

to remember that I am always counting on you.

I need you

to come to me when I call for you.

I need you

to forgive me for the stress I am sure
to cause you from time to time.

I need you . . .

to believe that one day I will be able to thank you
for all that you have done for me.

not to worry about your mistakes—I won't remember them.

not to worry about being perfect—I won't be either.

to remember that what I want to hear most is "I love you."

I need you

to remember that I like fun surprises.

I need you . . .

to take good care of yourself so that you'll have enough
energy to keep up with me.

to remember that I can't help having little
accidents now and then.

to understand that it would frighten me if you were
to get angry with me.

to make sure to save some time for yourself.

I need you

to believe that I love you as much as you love me.

I need you

to understand that it's okay to leave me as long as
you always come back for me.

I need you

to teach me how to play patty-cake.

I need you . . .

to make sure our home is safe for me.

to keep my baby book up to date.

to tuck me in at night with a kiss.

to teach me how to do the things I will
one day need to do for myself.

I need you

to remember how much I love to discover new things.

I need you . . .

to understand that people in costumes might scare me.

to give me all the affection you can muster.

to understand that some things have changed
since you were my age.

to love me the most when I don't seem to love you at all.

I need you

to make sure I have plenty of room to move around.

I need you

because without you I don't know what I'd do.

ACKNOWLEDGMENTS

I enjoy the support of many people, which is the only reason I am able to accomplish much of anything worthwhile. To them a heartfelt thanks is given—to Ron Pitkin, my publisher, and the staff at Cumberland House, including my editor, Lisa Taylor, who once again helped me to make this book the best it could be; to Julie Jayne, Stacie and Chris Bauerle, and Teresa Wright, thank you all; to my friend Janet Moran who took the photographs of these precious little faces; to Jill, my wife, for her unlimited support and encouragement, and finally to my beautiful daughter Meagan, who reminded me of what life was like when she was just a babe in arms slobbering on me.

TO CONTACT THE AUTHOR OR PHOTOGRAPHER

write in care of the publisher:

Cumberland House Publishing
431 Harding Industrial Drive
Nashville, TN 37211

or e-mail the author:

greg.lang@mindspring.com

or visit the photographer's web site:

www.oijoyphoto.com